Outreach and Identity: Evangelical Theological Monographs
World Evangelical Fellowship Theological Commission

Series Editor: Klaus Bockmuehl

No. 4   Evangelicals and Social Ethics

Evangelicals and Social Ethics

A Commentary on Article 5 of the Lausanne Covenant

Klaus Bockmuehl

Translated by David T. Priestley

InterVarsity Press
Downers Grove, Illinois 60515
United States of America

The Paternoster Press
Exeter, England

Originally published as Evangelikale Sozialethik: Der
Artikel 5 der "Lausanner Verpflichtung" © 1975
by Brunnen Verlag, Giessen und Basel

English translation © 1979 by Inter-Varsity Christian
Fellowship of the United States of America

InterVarsity Press is the book-publishing division
of Inter-Varsity Christian Fellowship.

Scripture quotations, unless otherwise noted,
are from the Revised Standard Version
of the Bible, copyrighted 1946, 1952, © 1971, 1973,
and used by permission.

CANADA: InterVarsity Press, 1875 Leslie Street, Unit 10,
Don Mills, Ontario M3B 2M5

AUSTRALIA: Emu Book Agencies, Pty., Ltd.,
63 Berry Street, Granville, 2142 N.S.W.

SOUTH AFRICA: Oxford University Press,
P.O. Box 1141, Cape Town

ISBN: 0-87784-491-7 (USA)
ISBN: 0-85364-261-3 (UK)

Made and printed in the United States of America for
InterVarsity Press, Downers Grove, IL 60515, and for the
Paternoster Press, Ltd., Paternoster House, 3 Mount
Radford Crescent, Exeter, Devon, by Malloy
Lithographing Inc., 5411 Jackson Road, Ann Arbor,
MI 48106; cover by Frank Prasel Graphics,
2205 Ashland, Evanston, IL 60201.

1

Social Ethics and the Lausanne Congress

The International Congress on World Evangelization in Lausanne (1974) elevated social ethics to a theme in its own right with three major lectures. These lectures addressed topics which later were worked over to become the social ethics article of the "Lausanne Covenant." Two of the lectures, those by the South Americans René Padilla and Samuel Escobar, were plenary addresses; the third, given by the senior figure of evangelical social ethics in the United States, Carl F. H. Henry, opened the sessions of a special committee for ethics and social ethics.

The plenary addresses had already been available in print to the participants six months before the Congress began. At the Congress itself, the speakers only gave synopses of their papers; the basic concerns were defined again and the objections which had been raised in the meantime by Congress participants were discussed. These second drafts were generally more sharply delineated than the original ones. Therefore, I shall base my analysis on them.

Under the title "Evangelism and the World," René Padilla, secretary for Latin America of the International Fellowship of

Evangelical Students, dealt with the need for evangelism to have concrete ethical results. Beginning with the term "comprehensive approach," propagated in the newer missiology and within the ecumenical movement, Padilla called for a comprehensive understanding of the concept and the task of evangelism. His slogan was "The whole Gospel for the whole man and for the whole world!" Jesus must be proclaimed as Lord as well as Savior.

This task of comprehensive proclamation, said Padilla, is concealed and hindered at this time by a false worldliness. As an example, he severely criticized North American "culture Christianity." The effect of accommodating Christianity to its surrounding culture is that while we may still be able to see individual sins, we cannot see the sins and the evil of society. This is so, precisely because we have adapted to it.

From the concept of "comprehensive evangelism" the necessity of the "prophetic office of the Church" (that is, the indictment of the evils of the social order) follows naturally, Padilla argued. This prophetic task must always go hand in hand with evangelism.

"Comprehensive evangelism," however, does not aim only at concrete repentance in society but necessarily with individuals as well. Still, there can be no concrete repentance without ethical instruction. Therefore, evangelism always must speak ethically, too; that is, it must be concerned with human behavior.

In many new ways Padilla explained that there can be no antithesis between loving God and loving one's neighbor, or between faith and works, eschatology and ethics, evangelism and ministry, conversion and social renewal. Nor can one differentiate between primary and secondary tasks in missions.

Samuel Escobar, then general secretary of Inter-Varsity Christian Fellowship in Canada, gave the second major address on the theme "Evangelism and Man's Search for Freedom, Justice and Fulfillment." Escobar extended Padilla's basic line into social ethics proper. Like Padilla, he stressed that evangelism cannot be only a sermon on individual salvation but must be a message of the kingdom of God; that is, it must include the Christian's moral obligations. Evidently, he considers a purely eschatological-future understanding of the Christian message of salvation, common among evangelical Christians, to be the main hindrance on the path to recovering an evangelical social ethic. Conversely, he exhorts us to do away with any alternative between eschatology and ethics.

In Escobar's opinion, the approach of evangelicals to ethics also is limited partly because they often concentrate strong efforts on evangelism (that is, on initial proclamation), but beyond that they neglect the continuing teaching and instruction. That naturally has lead to ethics, especially social ethics, being stunted.

In contrast, Jesus constantly had both these things in view: he preached the kingdom of God and he identified himself with the oppressed. We must conclude from that that a *spiritually* liberated person also has a concern for *earthly* liberation. Isaiah 61:1, the main motto of the Lausanne Congress ("proclaim liberty to the captives, and the opening of the prison to those who are bound"), the Scripture which Jesus repeated in his first sermon in Nazareth (Lk. 4:18), cannot be spiritualized in any way.

In Escobar's view of the ethical and social-ethical characteristics of evangelism, the church plays an important role. For him the church is both a prototype and an example of a new society. The church's solution of the slavery question and its conquest of racism should prove that, he thinks. The church in South America, through some of its ventures, has made an exemplary contribution toward land reform. In this context Escobar drew attention to the effect these social-ethical experiments had on evangelism in the narrower sense; where land reform was carried out the church grew also. Here the usual sequence of personal regeneration and its social consequences is reversed; where the social consequences are extended, we are told, the door is also open for evangelism.

This is the same idea that Emilio Castro, a South American who is now the director of the Department for Mission and Evangelism of the World Council of Churches in Geneva, put forward in his famous essay for the Geneva Conference on Church and Society (1966). There for the first time it was said that in certain situations political and economic liberation must precede the preaching of personal conversion and reconciliation with God.[1]

It seems that in Escobar's thought there are two elements standing side by side which are basically incompatible. He emphasizes that the church of Jesus is a special entity in the world and that the examples of how problems of human social life can be solved are possible only on the basis of the redemptive work of Christ. But if that is correct, then a prophetic demand on society is unfounded because the same condition does not apply to society in general. The claim of a "prophetic ministry" would then make sense only if it had a different content (perhaps based on a creation ethic) or if it presupposed universal redemption and based its ethical claim on society on it. So far as I can see, Escobar has not yet considered these difficulties.

He concluded his exposition with the significant comment that bloody revolutions have often been avoided where Christians fulfilled their social responsibility in time. He mentioned the far-reaching social reforms in Britain in the nineteenth century, which were initiated by conscious Christians like William Wilberforce and the Earl of Shaftesbury.

In the third lecture, "Christian Personal and Social Ethics in Relation to Racism, Poverty, War, and Other Problems," Carl F. H. Henry opened the deliberations of the commission (one of twenty-three) which addressed itself to the problem of ethics. At the second session of this committee Henry also presented an intensified synopsis of his concerns.

Henry combined, so to speak, Padilla's and Escobar's aims once more. The gospel, and with it evangelism, so he said, necessarily stands in relation to public life. The alteration of unjust social structures is a proper program for evangelicals. He substantiated this by referring, just as Escobar did, to Jesus' sermon in Nazareth (Is. 61; Lk. 4). According to it, the gospel we preach must also mean concrete good news for the oppressed and must be felt to be that as well.

Beyond that, Henry said, by his resurrection Jesus has overcome all powers of oppression, and through the church this victory is continued in the whole history of mankind. From this there follows for Henry both the "prophetic office of the church" (that is, the task of preaching, challenging and denouncing social injustice) and the practical effort toward just structures, laws and conduct. Demonstrations by Christians, for example, could be an expression of the prophetic office.

Henry also discussed the eschatological reservation which is often raised against social-ethical initiatives among evangelicals: in a fallen world justice cannot become a reality anyway. Henry responded that evangelism in this world is just as little able to completely succeed, and yet we are called to strive after it with every effort. Similarly we should put forth this kind of effort for social-ethical involvement which, even though relative and imperfect, could improve the living conditions of many people.

As much as one would like to follow Henry's theses and intentions, the reasons he gives are not convincing. Jesus' sermon in Nazareth proves that the new life presently is realized only very individually, not generally (only one widow in Zarephath and "only Naaman the Syrian" Lk. 4:26-27) and that it requires an acceptance accompanied by the conquest of pride which the population of Nazareth significantly had already declined. A social ethic cannot be based on Luke 4:18-19. The new life takes preliminary shape only in individual cases which certainly then will serve as an example and illumination.

The second reason which Henry gives is also uncertain. If he wants to say that the church is the realm of Christ's victory over the world, one could agree without hesitation. But he means more than that; he asserts that the victory of Christ is continued by the church.

This statement lacks precision. The church resembles the earthly Christ; it suffers, is persecuted and, nevertheless, wins individuals and single groups. It is, however, not yet the church victorious. Henry's claims demand more careful and circumspect theological substantiation.

In a night session, customary at such congresses, a subcommittee of the commission edited a final resolution which has been published with the other documents of the Lausanne Congress. The resolution clarifies various aspects of the commission's discussion of and attempt at furthering Henry's theses. The following points may give an indication of this:

1. Regeneration is the presupposition of all Christian social responsibility.

2. Sometimes the church, but more often the individual Christian or a group of Christians, is the agent of Christian action in society. Individuals or groups can take over specialized tasks which the church (as the whole of its offices and ministries) must not be asked to assume.

3. The negative task of indicting evil and injustice belongs to the "prophetic ministry of the church," but beyond that the church must come forward with positive, creative social-ethical teaching.

4. Even more, Christians are expected to exemplify and make Christian teaching a reality, as can be seen in William Wilberforce and others. Christians should be catalysts of social reform and renewal, light and salt of the earth, illuminating and preserving mankind.

5. For dealing with possessions the catchword is "stewardship." Concretely, that means that our possessions are entrusted to us so we may help others maintain life. "Help for self-help" takes precedence in this; "it is better to teach someone to fish than to give him a fish."

6. Christian social ethics also thinks of change for the better on the level of "structures," that is, laws and institutions. But such change must always take place only *with*, not *against*, the parties concerned, that is, "democratically." Here also Wilberforce gives examples by which we can orient ourselves.

7. The commission finally declared itself especially in favor of the efforts of the church to strengthen marriage and family and against pornography and any form of racism.

2
The Text of
Article 5

The text of Article 5 of the Lausanne Covenant on the social responsibility of Christians, which we will subsequently analyze, reads as follows:

We affirm that God is both the Creator and the Judge of all men. We therefore should share his concern for justice and reconciliation throughout human society and for the liberation of men from every kind of oppression. Because mankind is made in the image of God, every person, regardless of race, religion, color, culture, class, sex or age, has an intrinsic dignity because of which he should be respected and served, not exploited. Here too we express penitence both for our neglect and for having sometimes regarded evangelism and social concern as mutually exclusive. Although reconciliation with man is not reconciliation with God, nor is social action evangelism, nor is political liberation salvation, nevertheless we affirm that evangelism and socio-political involvement are both part of our Christian duty. For both are necessary expressions of our doctrines of God and man, our love for our neighbor and our obedience to Jesus Christ. The message of salvation implies also a message of judgment upon every form of alienation, oppression and discrimination, and we should not be afraid to denounce evil and injustice wherever they exist. When people receive Christ they are born again into his kingdom and must seek not only to exhibit but also to spread its righteousness in the midst of an unrighteous world. The salvation we claim should be transforming us in the totality of our personal and social responsibilities. Faith without works is dead. (Acts 17:26, 31; Gen. 18:25; Isa: 1:17; Psa. 45:7; Gen. 1:26, 27; Jas. 3:9; Lev. 19:18; Luke 6:27, 35; Jas. 2:14-26; John 3:3, 5; Matt. 5:20; 6:33; 2 Cor. 3:18; Jas. 2:20)

The Formation of the Text
A comparison of the proposed draft distributed at Lausanne with the final text in its various language versions leads to several significant observations.

To begin with, it should be noted that the article has changed its place in the sequence of themes treated by the Covenant. Originally, it stood in seventh place, after the sections on "the church and evangelism" and "cooperation in evangelism," that is, after two articles which developed the task of evangelism which Article 4 had talked about. In the final version the section on social responsibility is pushed further forward to follow immediately after the section on evangelism. So social responsibility is subordinated to, but at the same time associated with, evangelism.

The new position grants the article an importance similar to the task of proclamation; these two tasks of Christians are discussed before the first task, evangelism itself, is considered in detail.

In further comparison of the first and second drafts of the text a series of amplifications, clarifications and sharpenings of the original text can be noted.

1. The new text no longer speaks about our responsibility to be concerned about righteousness but characterizes righteousness as the concern of God himself. But God is also concerned with reconciliation and "the liberation of men from any kind of oppression." Here "liberation," the much-discussed catchword of ecumenical debate in recent years, is admitted into the text of the

Lausanne Covenant although it did not appear in the original draft. The same is true for the qualifying amplification "from every kind of oppression" which does not permit "liberation" to be understood only in the spiritual sense.

2. Disregarding minor corrections, the original demand to treat people with dignity has now been changed into a declaration which serves as the basis of the exhortation to treat them accordingly: "every person . . . has an intrinsic dignity." Initially, only the divine image in man, his likeness to God, was advanced as the reason that people should be treated appropriately, "for God's sake," so to speak. In the new version each person gains a value of his own, a dignity intrinsic to himself. To the original verbs, "served, not exploited," the new text has added the verb "respected."

3. Furthermore, the great fields of Christian activity—evangelism and social as well as political activity—are taken to be not only a necessary expression of our doctrines of God and man; the new text adds that both are also a part of our obligation as Christians and that both are motivated by "our obedience to Jesus Christ."

4. Probably more important than the previously mentioned amplifications of the original draft is the following proposition: from now on not only every kind of alienation and oppression but also "discrimination" is placed under God's judgment. Especially weighty is the new addition: "we should not be afraid to denounce evil and injustice wherever they exist." While the first version only spoke of an implicit (and therefore rather general) judgment upon evil in the preaching of the gospel, the final version urges more sharply the denunciation of particular, special forms in which evil appears.

5. Toward the end, the first version, which spoke only of the obligation to portray the righteousness of the kingdom of God in the midst of an unjust world, is expressly enlarged by the demand to "spread" this righteousness. The two last sentences of Article 5 are not contained in the first version at all. The list of Bible references is expanded appropriately by James 2:14-26 and the last two passages cited.

In summary, these three instances of an enlargement and/or

sharpening of the text are most significant: (1) the introduction of the term "liberation"; (2) the demand to "denounce" concrete evil conditions; and (3) the call to "spread" the righteousness of the kingdom of God. All these concepts were added to the text during the Congress.

The Structure of the Article

The present structure of the article is not completely clear. The article first deals with God's concern for righteousness which also must be ours as Christians. Second, it calls attention to human dignity and bases it on Christian anthropology.

The following part deals with the connection between evangelism and social involvement. It deplores the existing separation of the two, although it allows for their differences even as it stresses that both belong together. That in turn is substantiated dogmatically, theologically as well as anthropologically and ethically.

From the general evangelistic message of salvation Article 5 then infers the negative side and assigns Christians the task of delivering the message of judgment by "denouncing" concrete abuses.

One last segment urges the portrayal and spread of the righteousness of God's kingdom, substantiating this by alluding to regeneration and the necessary connection between faith and good works.

The following sequence of the material is also conceivable: (1) the connection between proclamation and service (as a demonstration of the connection between Articles 4 and 5); (2) the doctrine of God and social questions; (3) anthropology and social questions; (4) regeneration and its social significance; and (5) the negative (and the positive!) significance of the message of salvation for social life.

Even though the present sequence of material is somewhat unsatisfactory (the sentences on regeneration are rather tacked on behind and show that regeneration actually is not an integrated component of social ethics), yet the drafters of the article should be commended for giving a dogmatic reason for each of the various ethical demands. No ethic can succeed without motivation. Christian ethics presupposes it unconditionally.

3

The Social Responsibility of Christians: Nine Verbs of Action

Article 5 of the Lausanne Covenant presupposes, as we have seen, that there are two major areas of activity for Christians: evangelism as proclamation and social-political activity. The two are not identical in content, but neither may they be separated and isolated or set against each other.

On the basis of this presupposition, then, we shall examine the individual activities on the social side of Christian responsibility. This act-content is expressed in Article 5 by nine verbs: (1) share God's concern for justice; (2) share God's concern for reconciliation; (3) share God's concern for the liberation of men from every kind of oppression; (4) respect the dignity of every person; (5) exploit no one; (6) serve every person; (7) denounce evil and injustice; (8) seek to exhibit the righteousness of the kingdom of Christ; and (9) seek to spread the righteousness of the kingdom of Christ. In what follows I shall attempt to examine these social-ethical demands for their biblical roots, to define them more closely and, if necessary, to correct them.

1. Share God's Concern for Justice.
Isaiah 1:17 is cited as evidence: "Seek justice, correct oppression."

The deduction from the doctrine of God, as the text of the Lausanne Covenant has it, is correct: "[The Lord] executes justice for the oppressed" (Ps. 146:7).[2] The same statement is made about the Messiah: "He will bring forth justice to the nations. . . . He will faithfully bring forth justice" (Is. 42:1, 3).

Calling attention to God's conduct as a model or analogy, the Scripture also talks of man's realization of justice. It is above all the task of the king to create justice and righteousness, as is said of David (2 Sam. 8:15) and of Josiah (Jer. 22:15; compare Prov. 29:4: "By justice a king gives stability to the land"). Beyond that, however, it is the task of the whole nation to create justice. Therefore, the prophet Amos accuses the people of warping justice and demands that they restore the law.

Further clarification shows that concern for righteousness relates primarily to jurisprudence, court proceedings and the normal course of justice (see Amos 5:15: "Establish justice in the gate" and Hab. 1:4: "Justice goes forth perverted"). But also in social relations in the narrower sense, in business and commerce, there are unjust practices of the powerful against the poor; furthermore, such practices have been consolidated into unjust regulations and laws. On all three levels the people must seek to restore justice and righteousness: in courts, legislation and daily business with each other.

We notice that the quotations given—as well as the biblical quotations already attached to the article itself—are exclusively from the Old Testament, but with this alone the demand to establish earthly, social righteousness does have a sufficient biblical basis.

2. Share God's Concern for Reconciliation.

Both in the Old and the New Testament this word seems almost always to be used in reference to the reconciliation of man with God (see 2 Cor. 5:19-20, for example). The New Testament, however, speaks clearly about interpersonal reconciliation, particularly in two passages. In 1 Corinthians 7:11 divorcees who come under the influence of the gospel are encouraged to be reconciled even after a complete divorce. And in Matthew 5:23-24 Jesus commands that a person be reconciled with his brother before he makes his sacrifice.

Actually, however, neither passage talks about that reconciliation which God and with him the Christian want to effect. Here it is still a matter of self-reconciliation, that is, a case in which one is involved himself.[3]

Nevertheless, there is one passage, which admittedly is worded differently but seems directly to support the point made by this article: Jesus' statement in Matthew 5:9: "Blessed are the peacemakers, for they shall be called sons of God." In the previously mentioned central passages regarding the readiness of Jesus' disciples to be reconciled, reconciliation is the Christian alternative to enmity and hate. The setting of the word in the context of Jesus' radicalization of the commandments in his Sermon on the Mount indicates that reconciliation is nothing less than the positive fulfillment of the prohibition, "You shall not kill." But in the beatitude Jesus goes beyond even that when he calls the person "blessed" who builds bridges and makes peace between others, saying that he most resembles the heavenly Father.

The New Testament, nevertheless, sets limits on readiness to conciliate. One is not to reconcile oneself to wickedness (see Eph. 5:7, 11; 1 Cor. 5:9; 2 Thess. 3:6) and false doctrine (Rom. 16:17; Tit. 3:10; 2 Jn. 10). Instead one should separate himself from both according to the Lord's rule (Mt. 18:15-17).

3. Share God's Concern for Liberation of Men from Every Kind of Oppression.

"Liberation"—the New Testament speaks of this catchword of the ecumenical social-ethical discussion current today in another (spiritual) sense. It speaks of the "freedom" for which "Christ has set us free" (Gal. 5:1; see Col. 1:13; Jn. 8:36). Moreover, the stress lies on God or Christ as the agent of this liberation. That is also the case for the Zechariah's eulogy which is a favorite quote concerning "liberation": "delivered from the hand of our enemies" (Lk. 1:74). Similarly, in 2 Timothy 4:16-17 Paul ascribes his rescue from his lawsuit to God himself, since everyone else had deserted him.

In regard to earthly liberation perhaps one might think of 1 Corinthians 7:21 where Paul says on the question of civil self-liberation of the slaves, "If you can gain your freedom, avail yourself of the opportunity." The meaning of the passage, however, is uncertain enough that Goodspeed and the margins of the Revised Standard Version and the New English Bible translate the idea virtually in the opposite way: "But if you can gain your freedom, make use of your present condition instead." This translation probably also fits the context which mentions that in faith status doesn't matter anymore; a slave is free in Christ, and a free man is a slave of Christ.[4] So this passage could hardly provide the foundation for a far-reaching program of liberation.

The motto of the Lausanne Congress ("proclaim liberty to the captives, and the opening of the prison to those who are bound," Is. 61:1 and Lk. 4:18), as we have briefly indicated already, is probably just as unsuitable. We have seen what Padilla, Escobar and Henry attribute to these words. Basically, they want to make liberating action in a social sense (that is, the social ministry element) not only a part of "mission," as John Stott confirmed in his opening address in Lausanne as the conclusion of recent discussion; they want to make it an area within "evangelism" itself. Thus, Carl Henry expressly said: this is a matter of evangelism. Indeed, together with his South American friends here he comes close to the proposition which Article 5 of the Lausanne Covenant rejected: political liberation is also salvation; social action is also evangelism.

Article 5 takes up the catchword "liberation" but does not quote Isaiah 61:1 and Luke 4:18, and justifiably so. These verses do not belong to the foundation of the social responsibility of Christians. The characteristic note is that freedom is to be *preached to* the captives; in Nazareth itself no kind of concrete liberation of prisoners, who most certainly would have been there, took place.

The particularism of Jesus' speech (which soon enough provoked the Nazarenes!) also should caution us against a social-ethical application of these verses. What he preached actually occurred but, like all prophets' works, only in *individual* cases as a prophetic anticipation of the end time. So already the words of Isaiah 61 were a proclamation of comfort addressed to a people in bondage, a *promise* which takes the year of jubilee (Lev. 25) as a parable of God's future action for his people.

Even when Christ says, "Today this scripture has been fulfilled in your hearing" (Lk. 4:21), it is impossible to understand that as a universal reality generally evident. Jesus did not empty the prisons. So this word of Jesus is probably to be understood primarily spiritually, or as a reference to the certainly numerous but nevertheless individual liberations of such people as were bound by sickness and demons. Neither Isaiah 61:1 nor Luke 4:18, 21 is a suitable foundation for social ethics, our earthly conduct.

It is the same for the other, related concept which might come into consideration here as lexically suitable, the Greek sozein, soteria (save, redeem). In ancient times the word was used for an act of the gods.[5] Human helpers and lifesavers are the king, a statesman or a doctor, once even a philosopher who "freed" people inwardly. In the Old Testament the judges could be such "redeemers" of their people. Salvation was accomplished by the intervention of a strong man in battle or in litigation. Both can also be said of God.

The word, though, does not signify self-rescue, self-liberation. In the context of its usage, actually, the deeper awareness is stressed that in the last analysis help is not to be expected from earthly power, from men or princes at all; the attitude of believers is always described as being still and trustfully waiting on God's intervention. Whoever seeks to help himself by his own hand falls into guilt (1 Sam. 25:26-28). But God can send real salvation.

In the New Testament we find "save" in an earthly sense only as salvation from danger on the waters (the quieting of the storm: Mt. 8:26; compare 14:30 and Acts 27) or as healing of sickness, that is, in cases of acute danger to physical life. Beyond that it is used only in a strict theological sense—as a redemption from man's present entanglement in sin or from the tribulation of the last days.

J. C. Hoekendijk, the great advocate of ecumenical social ethics, quite consciously adopted the Old Testament concept of shalom for the theological undergirding of earthly peace efforts; the New Testament soteria is not suited to it.[6]

Precisely the same recognition lies behind the statement of Article 5 which says that political liberation is not the same as salvation. John Stott in his introductory address in Lausanne made the relationship clear when he said, "Salvation is moral, not material." Salvation is from sin, not from injury. Stott sees, however, that the concepts "salvation," "rescue" and "liberation" have the same spiritual content in the New Testament and, therefore, wants to consider "liberation" as a practical modern alternative term for "salvation," which has become somewhat old-fashioned. Obviously, to avoid general confusion, it then should not be used at the same time for social processes.

Stott, however, is not consistent here. He himself said that we "must strive for humanization, development, wholeness, liberation and righteousness." But that kind of salvation, he said, is not yet salvation in the biblical sense.

In fact, in the future if we use the term we must clearly distinguish between two meanings of "liberation." For if the New Testament itself uses the concept theologically (with the God-relation in mind), the interest in earthly liberation (within interpersonal relations) can nevertheless be substantiated directly from the Old Testament.

Thus, for example, the Pentateuch specifies—certainly a special case—that the Israelite slave is to be set free in the Sabbath year (Ex. 21:2). Indeed, his owner, as a remembrance that he was himself once a slave in Egypt, must even give him presents to take with him into freedom (Deut. 15:12-14).

Jeremiah 34 talks of the same demand for liberation; there perfidious owners emancipate their servants when they are threatened but enslave them again as soon as the menace is past.

Isaiah 58:6, however, is the most important verse, a passage which the Lausanne Covenant might well have quoted: " ... to loose the bonds of wickedness, to undo the thongs of the yoke, to let the oppressed go free, and to break every yoke." This text stands in the context of other "physical deeds of mercy." Isaiah 58 is an extremely important chapter for social ethics, just as in the New Testament Matthew 25:31-46 parallels its thrust. Nevertheless, a difference of content may be observed. Beside providing for food, home, clothing and shelter, Matthew adds taking responsibility for fellowship, that is, visiting the sick and imprisoned; Isaiah adds the taking the responsibility to grant freedom.

So concern for liberation is biblically based. At the same time we must certainly emphasize the additional observation that the demand for freedom each time is directed *to the rulers or to the people as a whole,* insofar as they are able to bind or to free others. The legislation of the Pentateuch as well as the prophetic demands are addressed to the owners, to those who have the power. This statement will be confirmed further.

Philemon 16 is probably a New Testament parallel to the prophetic demand for freedom in Isaiah 58, even though it does not deal with a claim directed to the public but with a tactfully expressed request, person to person. Paul admonishes Philemon to amiably receive again his runaway slave Onesimus who has also become a Christian in the meantime, yet no longer only as a slave but as a brother in Christ and, beyond that, not only on the level of the church but also "in the flesh," that is, civilly. That can mean nothing other than that Paul wished Philemon would also outwardly liberate his fellow Christian. Here again the owner is addressed. Emancipation of others, not self-liberation, is the biblical view.

4. Respect the Dignity of Every Person.
Article 5 of the Lausanne Covenant substantiates the intrinsic worth of the person by referring to the image of God in man, a dignity derived from the original creation (Gen. 1:26-27). It could be added, according to Genesis 1:28, that the value of man is also based upon God's blessing. James supports his admonition to bridle the tongue with this notion of the dignity of man; critical talk about others violates their God-given dignity (Jas. 3:9).

Psalm 8:4 also belongs here: "What is man that thou [Lord] art mindful of him . . . ?" despite his so obvious lowliness. Psalm 8:5 says, "Yet thou . . . dost crown him with glory and honor." That is why people now possess honor, that is, have a "claim on recognition,"[7] despite their notorious frailty. God has blessed them.

Likewise, in the New Testament we find passages which deal primarily with the honor of God but also numerous others which safeguard the honor of man. In Matthew 5:22 and 39 (to which Adolf Schlatter refers)[8] Jesus intentionally radicalizes the prohibition of murder when he says you shall not despise another and belittle his worth. Generally the New Testament says to endure abuse yourself but not to abuse others, to be anxious not about your own honor but rather about that of your neighbor. Father and mother are to be honored (according to Ex. 20:12 and Mal. 1:6 as well as Mt. 15:4-5); likewise, the elderly (Lev. 19:32; Lam. 5:12). The servant should honor his master; the husband, his wife; the church, its elders (1 Tim. 6:1; 1 Pet. 3:7; 1 Tim. 5:17). Respect for rulers is laid on all (1 Pet. 2:17).

In summary, honor those to whom honor is due (Rom. 13:7). But from a Christian perspective that is now not simply those in higher places but, as a logical consequence of what was said above, every person: "Honor all men" (1 Pet. 2:17).

The relations of church members with each other show especially how much this is a Christian attitude. "Outdo one another in showing honor" (Rom. 12:10); and "in humility count others better than yourselves" (Phil. 2:3). Just as strongly, honor for false motives—often so tempting—is to be averted; James addresses himself against the false respect of the rich (2:1-4) and the educated (3:13-18; compare 1 Cor. 3:18-21).

Karl Barth summarizes three motives for honoring one's neighbor: (1) the creaturely honor (according to Ps. 8); (2) the added dignity of human beings which consists in the fact that Christ died for them (Rom. 14:15; 1 Cor. 8:11); and (3) the special honor due to man as he is called to the service of God (Jn. 12:26; 2 Cor. 3:9).[9] All three reasons derive man's honor from God. God's gift is the basis for human honor. Denial of God will destroy human honor.

5. Exploit No One.

"Learn to do good; seek justice" (Is. 1:17). This passage, which was cited earlier by the authors in support of Article 5, itself relates to a stipulation of the Pentateuch: "You shall not oppress a stranger" (Ex. 23:9). The commandment is supported by a reference to the fact that Israel herself was once a stranger in Egypt. The sentence stands in the context of the legal stipulations against oppressing the socially weak (on this theme, see Ex. 22:21-24 and Lev. 19:33-34).

In addition to the stranger, we find that widows, orphans and the poor are constantly mentioned as groups who are in danger of

' being exploited. The God of Israel, therefore, especially remembers to care for them, and to do so even by means of giving the Law. Ezekiel 22:29 shows the actualization of that danger: "The people of the land have practiced extortion and committed robbery; they have oppressed the poor and needy, and have extorted from the sojourner without redress" (see also v. 7).

Exodus 22 in this context mentions a series of concrete forms of exploitation. Exploitation, for example, is:

—harming the poor who must borrow, by charging compound interest (v. 25; compare the prohibition of charging interest within the community of Israel, Deut. 23:19-20; Lev. 25:36-37);

—withholding his clothing in the evening (in order to make the interest period longer?) from someone who has given it as surety but wants to redeem it after receiving his day's wages; it is the "only covering" of the poor (v. 27);

—perverting justice against the weak (Deut. 24:17, 19);

—sweatshop wages, delayed payment of wages (in order to force a few more interest points?), an evil decried in many socially critical chapters of the Old Testament (Deut. 24:14; Lev. 19:13; Jer. 22:13; compare Jas. 5:4);

—complete harvest of the fields, fruit trees and vineyards (Deut. 24:19-21), which means obstructing a source of food for the poorest for the sake of personal gain.

Further examples of exploitation, which threaten deportation of the nation into exile, are given in Amos 8:4-6 and 2:6-7: fraudulent weights and measures in the food business, reduction of the quality of goods for the sake of higher profits, arbitrary price increases, and all other means of self-enrichment by wronging one's neighbor,[10] again including perverting the law (Amos 5:12, 15).

Ezekiel 22 considers the princes and the rich of the land, above all, as exploiters. They go among the people like ravenous wolves to destroy life if only they can make a profit from it. The prophet thinks especially of the unscrupulous accumulation of real estate which flies in the face of God's law in Israel. But "her prophets have daubed for them with whitewash" (v. 28); the advocates of God's law made themselves the lackeys of vested interest.

The motive behind both those who actually exploit and those

who justify the exploitation is *pleonexia*, the greed and avarice which the New Testament together with uncleanness condemns as a cardinal sin and as idolatry.[11]

6. Serve Every Person.

The verb "serve" comes into the Lausanne Covenant from John Stott's major speech at the beginning of the Congress. Stott there makes it the main verb for mission; mission is service patterned after Jesus' example, comprising evangelism and *diakonia*.

"Service" is an exceptionally central concept for New Testament ethics, so central that Schlatter with good reason did not talk anymore about "Christian ethics" but of the "service of the Christian."[12]

The basis for service, in turn, is a Christological one; Christ himself is the one who "came not to be served but to serve" (Mt. 20:28). The Lord ministers as a servant; he will even wait on the table of the trustworthy servant after his work is done (Lk. 12:37). That is a promise for the future.

Proceeding from Jesus' ministry, service became a characteristic of the church of Jesus already in the pre-Easter period. Peter's mother-in-law, just healed, "served him" (Mt. 8:15). Likewise, the women from Galilee "provided for" the disciples with their resources (Lk. 8:3). Martha in Bethany is a further example (Jn. 12:2).

The time after Pentecost saw the introduction of special deacons ("those who serve tables") for the material provision of the believers; this, like the previously mentioned passages, shows the content of "ministry." In Acts 6, as in Matthew 10 where the twelve were commissioned, service is a further activity beside proclamation and teaching, that is, beside the "ministry of the Word." Both belong together.

Ministry and service, however, are not only the business of individuals but the general task of the church. "Through love be servants of one another," Paul writes to the Galatians (5:13). It is a labor of love to serve the saints in the name of God (Heb. 6:10). "Each in accordance with his special gift" should exercise this service, so that an entire stewardship and household of cooperative activities develop.

Everyone therefore shares in ministry in the Christian church. Where "serve" becomes the basic word for ethics, there can no longer be two classes, the rulers and the servers, an astonishing solution for the cardinal problem of society.

As a synonym to serving, Jesus' word to "do good" (Mk. 3:4) can certainly also be included.[13]

Looking back into the Old Testament contributes to a further definition of the content of "serving." First of all, it shows that the double definition of Article 5 ("serve not exploit") is biblical; in many passages already quoted under the term "exploitation" service also appears as its positive counterpart. Biblical ethics always adds positive command to negative prohibition.

That is true, for example, for relations with the stranger. Leviticus 19:34 (quite pertinent to the foreign-worker question of our day) admonishes not only not to exploit the stranger but also demands that "the stranger who sojourns with you shall be to you as the native among you." In fact, Leviticus continues, "You shall love him as yourself." In saying this Leviticus uses a verb which exceeds service and expresses preferential treatment, not merely benevolent neutrality.

The theological basis given for this is powerful: the Lord "loves the sojourner, giving him food and clothing" (Deut. 10:18). The equalization of the foreign worker demanded by the synod of the Evangelical Church in Germany in November 1974, therefore, has the best of biblical reasons. What was law in Israel in this regard commends itself to all nations.

Leviticus 19:34 is especially important for another reason. It deals with a demand for a supra-individual, structural order which the collective supports and which law makes reality; that is, it deals with social ethics in the strict sense, not only with individual ministry. But this general new regulation of residential rights for foreigners is surpassed by the biblical command to love, to *love the stranger*. This goes beyond the competence of law.

Likewise, the well-known chapter about the Sabbath-year laws (Lev. 25) provides an instructive definition of the content of service to one's neighbor. "And if your brother becomes poor, and cannot maintain himself with you, you shall maintain him; as a stranger and a sojourner he shall live with you. Take no interest from him or increase, but fear your God; that your brother may live beside you. ... You shall not rule over him with harshness" (Lev. 25:35-36, 43). The motivation for the expected behavior is the fear of God. Fear of God helps the weaker neighbor live; it holds greed in check. Humaneness presupposes God!

The content of service is here rendered with the word "maintain" ("relieve" KJV = strengthen, set securely, hold by the hand). Service serves to guarantee our neighbor's existence. Serving means to make it our duty to maintain the life of our neighbor.

Guarantee of existence, maintenance of life as an aim of *diakonia* (service), agrees with the positive instructions which Ezekiel 18:7-9, 13 and 16 contrast with the prohibition against exploitation: you should help the needy get food and clothing.

This leads us again to the demands of Isaiah 58. Beside proclaiming liberation, this chapter orders provisions for the basic needs of human existence: food, clothing, dwelling and the guarantee of law and social participation (see Mt. 25:31-46 and Jas. 2). That is the content of Christian service. It is a matter of maintaining life, one might almost say "first aid," as Jesus makes clear in his parable of the good Samaritan which illustrates his conception of neighbor love. In both Leviticus 25 and Luke 10 love consists in concrete service of support and of maintenance of life.

7. Denounce Evil and Injustice.

This formulation marks the first point at which Article 5 of the Lausanne Covenant, in my view, deviates from the message of the Bible. At the same time it deals with the area which possessed central importance for the social-ethical speeches at the Lausanne Congress, namely, with the so-called "prophetic office of the church."

Stating in advance the conclusion of our investigation, it is in fact correct that the prophets' message of salvation is accompanied with a message of judgment. The prophetic books of the Old Testament contain not a few sermons of judgment. Looked at biblically, the proclamation always has a double form: it speaks of God's "yes" to people and his "no" to sin. But "denounce" is not a biblically legitimate expression. To denounce (from the Latin root *denuntiare)* means to accuse, to expose to shame, to brand, and to do it in front of third parties. Likewise denounce (compare, "denunciation") clearly connotes negative information about a person or a situation, given to a third party, for example, the police. The ring of denigration in it is unmistakable.

An orientation in the structure of prophetic sermons of judgment with the help of some prominent chapters in Scripture produces another picture. If we consider such chapters as Isaiah 1 and 58, Jeremiah 7, 26 and 34 (the breach of faith in the year of release), Amos 4 as well as Matthew 3 (the sermon of John the Baptist, the last pre-Christian prophet) and even Matthew 21:13 (the words of Jesus at the cleansing of the temple) and Matthew 23 (the sevenfold woe against the scribes and Pharisees) the following pattern for the prophetic sermon of judgment comes to light:

1. The Word of God by the mouth of the prophets is addressed to the guilty themselves; it is a *personal address.* Characteristic of this is the constant recurrence of the second person plural, occasionally the singular: "you." Auditors of the prophetic preaching are the king of Israel (or the king and his advisors), single groups of the ruling class (the princes, the priests), the official prophets or even the whole people ("O Israel ... you ... , " Hos. 9:1). Occasionally an individual is addressed by name, as in the announcement of judgment to Shemaiah (Jer. 29:24-28), who thwarted Jeremiah's sermon on repentance. But even in this case the prophetic talk of judgment is not "denunciation," but a direct address to the guilty. The sermon of the prophet Nathan to David to repent ("You are the man," 2 Sam. 12:7) and of John the Baptist to King Herod ("It is not lawful for you to have" your brother's wife, Mt. 14:4) shows the same pattern. In this peculiarity of the prophets' sermons of judgment and repentance, therefore, we find the first criterion for the "prophetic office of the church."

2. It is *God,* who speaks through the prophets (Is. 56; Jer. 26). The people should "hear the word which the LORD speaks to you" (Jer. 10:1). Where God still talks to people through prophets, he addresses them personally and calls them to repent.

3. Then follows the description of the sins of the people (Is.

59; Jer. 7:8-11; 23:9-11), even in the form of a call of woes (for example, Jer. 22:13-14; 23:1; Amos 5:1) but again in a direct address; you have done so-and-so and are guilty.

4. The accusation goes on to threaten or announce the punishment (for example, Amos 8:7-14; Is. 23:13). But that is not the end of the prophetic speeches of judgment. At the end, rather, stands the fifth element in the pattern.

5. An appeal for change, a demand for repentance, a call back to God and his commandments, close the sermons. Only where this call finds no hearing must God's judgment be carried out. Even in the desperate situation which necessitates the message of judgment, God shows the people the way out open to them. "Amend your ways and your doings, and I will let you dwell in this place" (Jer. 7:3). Yes, in the midst of the repentance sermon, the demand to do good and promise of blessing can have a place (Is. 58). This shows that it is not a person enraged by human badness but the sovereign God who determines the prophetic word and who must determine the "prophetic office of the church" today also.

In summary, prophetic preaching is done by order of the Highest: "Declare to my people their transgression, to the house of Jacob their sins" (Is. 58:1). It is done in direct address as an accusation to the sinner not as denunciation to some third party. Not only the formal criterion of the second person ("you") but also the theological standard that the prophetic judgment sermon includes the call to repentance confirms this. Prophetic preaching is done on the basis of God's command and prohibition and with the announcement of blessing and curse. The prophet conveys the Word, but God will bring about the tangible consequences.

The New Testament confirms these findings. John the Baptist, for example, addressed himself directly to the Pharisees and the people ("You brood of vipers!" Mt. 3:7) with a threat of punishment, a call to repentance and a description of the right conduct. He also addressed the ruler Herod individually in direct speech instead of demeaning him to his subjects.

There is a seeming exception to the rule. In Matthew 23, it is true, Jesus first addresses the people with his accusation against scribes and Pharisees; but in 23:13 as his speech goes on he significantly shifts to the direct address with the sevenfold woe ("Woe to you . . . ").[14]

It is this exercise of the direct address which leads the Baptist as well as Jesus into the suffering which, since Old Testament times, has been "an integral part of prophetic service."[15] The prophetic office of the church is the public "accusation on the basis of law and Gospel"[16] (even for Stephen, Acts 7); it consists of a directly addressed accusation and call to repentance.

To "denounce" to the public may be fashionable, but it is not biblical. The other, really prophetic way, has been little traveled in recent times.[17] There can only be a denunciation of the sin to the sinner himself. Perhaps that is the meaning of the verb in Article 5.

8. Seek to Exhibit the Righteousness of the Kingdom of Christ.
The eighth and ninth formulations of Christian conduct which pertain to social-ethical responsibility expect the regenerate to seek to exhibit and spread the righteousness of the kingdom of God into which they have been introduced by their rebirth.

The text of the article puts the relativizing verb "seek" in front of "exhibit" and "spread." The intent of this insertion, which wants to avoid the sound of obvious ethica gloriae with a note of restraint, is praiseworthy. The verb selected is less so. For it gives rise to the impression that Christian ethics (emphasizing here Christian ethics, with regeneration presupposed!) is a matter of endeavor, exertion and effort of which man is the agent. But that would be to turn our gaze in an entirely false direction. Another formulation, such as "it is the calling of Christians to exhibit the righteousness of the kingdom of God" or something similar, would not give rise to errors of this sort so easily.

We now turn to the actual statement. To "exhibit" means to present, expose, show, give an example, something like a sample, a product, a pattern, a model. "Pattern" and "model" would be good approximations for what Christian ethics deals with.

Perhaps the text of the article simply means "make real the righteousness of the kingdom of God." That also fits the Latin concept exhibere behind the English word. Its slight tone of "hold forth" coincides with the New Testament interest in the realization of faith in the behavior of the believer. For in the New Testament "ethics," following Jesus, also deals with the inward becoming outward, something perceptible, existing tangibly. The newly planted tree (Jesus' simile for the regenerated person addressed in this article) should bring forth fruit from within itself.

The parable of tree and fruit helps convey a basic understanding of this point of doctrine. It can be interpreted from two sides. On the one hand, the interest in the fruit, the results, must be emphasized. The parable obviously presupposes that one plants a tree or lays out a vineyard in order to obtain fruit (Is. 5:2: "he looked for it to yield grapes"). Repeatedly, the New Testament says that preaching and faith have their goal in the conduct of the believer. Not only does James say, "Faith apart from works is barren" (2:20); Paul also aims for a "faith working through love" (Gal. 5:6). Faith must "become effectual" (Philem. 6, KJV). We must agree with Padilla's thesis that the gospel always aims at an ethically significant realization in the life of the person.

A little word, which is quite distinctive of Paul's way of thinking because of its frequent appearance testifies to this mode of thinking. It is the Greek *hina*, the conjunction which introduces the concluding statement that shows the intention, purpose and objective of an undertaking. It appears in the central New Testament passages which connect God's work of salvation with the life of man, or more exactly, which demonstrate that God's saving work has its significance precisely in the person's new conduct. 2 Corinthians 5:15, for example, says that Christ "died for all, that [*hina*] those who live might live no longer for themselves but for him who for their sake died and was raised." Romans 6:4 says that "we were buried therefore with him by baptism into death, so that [*hina*] ... we too might walk in newness of life." Titus 2:14 talks about Christ, "who gave himself for us to [*hina*] redeem us from all iniquity and to purify for himself a people of his own who are zealous for good deeds."

Those are only a few examples among many. They all make clear that God's saving work is not an end in itself but aims at the new life, the good works of the Christian, and attains its goal only in them. It therefore follows that the horizon of dogmatics is "ethics"; furthermore, that Christian mission and evangelism dare never be directed simply toward awakening faith and hope or simply toward church planting and church growth. Rather the goal must be the goal of 2 Corinthians 5:15; Romans 6:4 and Titus 2:14, in other words, that more and more people would do God's will.

This intentionality, this goal-orientation, however, is not a part of regular instruction in Protestantism. The Lutheran Reformation, with very good reason (medieval ideas of man's self-justification by good works), sought to emphasize the other side of the interpretation of the parable of the tree and fruit. It surely needs also to be stressed constantly that there must be a previous inner renewal of the nature of man if there is to be any manifestation of that new nature. God's action must precede all human action, or there will be no worthy human conduct. The one side emphasizes the aim; the other, the source.

Martin Luther, in reference to the parable of tree and fruit, liked to emphasize (and with definite exegetical justification) that where the new planting is made it indubitably will bear fruit. He conceived the relationship principally as consecutive, not as purposive; he saw the fruit as a quasi-natural-automatic result of the new planting and not so much as its intention. His followers have intensified this tendency almost into mutually exclusive opposites so that recent handbooks of dogmatics originating in Lutheranism emphatically deny the idea of intentionality toward a new life in terms of ethics.

From the history of theology we know that Luther's explanation that good works were the natural consequence of faith met with quiet skepticism even among Luther's own followers. For them faith serves primarily in comforting the weak conscience. Therefore, in this view, the uncomfortable question whether fruits of faith accompany new life is to be rejected. It might jeopardize the certainty of faith. For this view it is suspect to understand regeneration as a moral renewal of man (as Luther's interpretation of the parable of tree and fruit still said). Faith is only the hand which grasps the grace of forgiveness but no longer active faith as in the first years of the Reformation. Then ethics, which the Bible views as ultimately inevitable, again becomes a matter of subsequent, artificial exhortation; it slips back into legalism.

In contrast to this the New Testament designates the new life of the Christian as the goal of God's saving work. It is, however, an intention which is also a consequence, a consequence which results from God's saving work and does not exist without it.

Neither of the two sides of the interpretation of the parable of tree and fruit, therefore, may properly be held without the other. The relation of planting and fruit is a *consecutive-purposive* one. In that other central passage of New Testament soteriology (Eph. 2:10), in fact, this very conclusion is expressed by the concise, pertinent, unsurpassable formula: saved not *by* works but *for* good works. Salvation, on the one hand, is the condition of good works; on the other hand, it is the gateway into good works to which the believers are actually, as it literally says, "predestined," appointed. The fruit of good works (these external, noticeable evidences of the inner, invisible renewal of man, this incarnation of faith) should be the result as long as we live in the flesh (Phil. 1:22).[18]

It is this biblical *concept* which the Lausanne Covenant expresses with the word "exhibit." But also the *term* "to exhibit," if it is interpreted as "make known," "show," "make real," "make visible," is supported by scriptural evidence. The righteousness of the kingdom of Christ is to be made visible by his disciples. Consider Matthew 5:16: "Let your light so shine before men, that they may see your good works and give glory to your Father who is in heaven." "Let them see" is the same as "show."

Ephesians 5:8 and 9 says something quite similar: "Once you were darkness, but now you are light in the Lord; walk as children of light." Immediately afterwards the apostle Paul talks about righteousness, goodness and truth, all of which should be realities in the life of believers.

The apostle James is thinking in the same direction when he asks, "Who is wise . . . among you?" and answers, "By his good life let him *show* his works in the meekness of wisdom" (3:13).

The most direct and instructive parallel to Matthew 5:16, however, is probably the statement in the first letter of Peter: "Maintain good conduct among the Gentiles, so that[19] . . . they may see your good deeds and glorify God on the day of visitation" (2:12). What is noticeable will one day be noticed. 1 Peter 3:16 also figures that where Christians with good consciences lead good lives the antagonists themselves, who may for a time have spoken ill of what is good, will someday be convinced and see.

Again today the concept of visibility of good works is rarely found in textbooks of Christian theology. The related Scripture passages simply do not appear in the Bible reference indexes of the great ethicists.

To the good works which they set as the Christian's goal these verses add yet a *finis finalis,* a last, transcendent goal: the honor of God and the conquest of unbelief. In the Reformation confessions that goal was still taken for granted as a part of doctrine.[20]

In fact, there is good reason to assume that the idea that faith is shown by conduct also played a prominent role in early Christian catechizing and admonition.[21] Christians were (and are) actually being observed by those around them. Since the life of the non-Christian is sick and torn with inner contradictions, the life of the Christian, whose contradictions are healed, must be a recognizable sign of healing. In this regard, Peter thought that wives would persuade their unbelieving husbands without words, by their conduct alone (1 Pet. 3:1). Such husbands would then have a visible witness. Mainstream Protestant, systematic theology has done little to encourage asking about the noticeable effects of the new life from God; in fact, we have been restrained from asking the question. Nevertheless, our exegetical teachers have felt confronted with this question again and again and this has helped to disturb our confident dogmatic security. Thus Schlatter writes, "It is the goal of Jesus and his disciples that through them God's greatness would become visible and praise to God might arise among men."[22] Joachim Jeremias also says, "In the life of the disciples the victory of God's sovereignty should become perceptible."[23]

The expositors of the first letter of Peter, by the way, presume that the admonitions for an exemplary life were given from the viewpoint of the missionary obligation of the church. Here lay (and lies) a special possibility for the church to preach under persecution. "During defamation and oppression the life of Christians becomes the most prominent means of mission. The world shall get to see what it does not want to hear."[24]

So these passages from 1 Peter are a new confirmation of the necessity of linking verbal preaching and preaching by life; the church fulfills its mission with both. In civil life, in business life, in marriage, not only in brotherly relations, praiseworthy works should be exercised,[25] with the ultimate purpose of God's glorification.

Letting the fruits of the kingdom of God be seen invites non-Christians to infer the roots from the fruits, the cause from the effect. The answer Jesus sent to the questioning Baptist bears the same form. Jesus did not directly answer that he was the one for whom John waited; instead he described what he was doing. With the concluding sentence, "blessed is he who takes no offense at me" (Mt. 11:6), he invited the Baptist himself to draw the proper conclusion about the doer from the deeds.

This recalls the picture which Karl Barth drew in 1920, before he plunged into the whirlpool of "dialectical theology" for a decade and maintained the principle of non-perceptibility of the effects of God's works upon man. Then he wrote regarding the dispute over the revelation of Jesus that if he saw the enormous historical effects which the appearance of Jesus through his apostles has had upon the entire ancient world, then he would certainly presume an unusually ponderous cause; just as the spreading ripples of a pond would indicate that a stone had been thrown into it, even when he had not seen the stone.[26]

The effects testify to the cause. So the gospel now intends this very rule to apply in the analogous area of Christian discipleship. This is no different from applying to the church itself the rule which Jesus gave for the judgment of false teachers and prophets:[27] "You will know them by their fruits" (Mt. 7:16, 20). That is no more than right. Good works are, as Billy Graham said in his opening address at Lausanne, "the evidence," the "proof" of faith.

The area of ethics is, therefore, continuously of great significance for mission. Non-Christians will keep in mind (and who would blame them for it?) James's fundamental statement, "show your wisdom by your walk" (Jas. 3:13), and make Christian practice the standard for judging the message. Therefore, Schlatter concludes, "There is considerable cause that always, perhaps mainly, the truth of Christianity is measured by its ethics. Therefore, a sound ethic, so far as it does not remain only theory, belongs to the necessary equipment of the church if its evangelism and mission is to succeed."[28]

"Exhibit the righteousness of the kingdom of Christ": the importance (or lack of it!) which large segments of the dogmatic tradition of Protestantism has assigned this matter has required a detailed discussion of this one verb, "exhibit." For the question of social ethics, like that of every other ethic, is basically superfluous if we deny the necessity, or even the possibility, of making the righteousness of the kingdom of God visible and known.

9. Seek to Spread the Righteousness of the Kingdom of Christ.
The last demand is that in the midst of an unjust world we should not only exhibit but also spread the righteousness of the kingdom of God. By this we understand that the realization of this righteousness in one's own life is not enough; rather, we should take an interest in seeing that it be realized increasingly elsewhere.

In itself the expression "spread" in the context with the "righteousness of the kingdom of Christ" arouses misgivings. True, talk about "spreading the kingdom" is familiar to us. Evangelicals like to use it; and it is found also in the flowering of the mission-theology literature at the end of the nineteenth century in which mission itself was conceived as the "spreading of the kingdom of God."

Pivotal idioms of this kind usually come from the language of the Bible. But that does not seem to apply to this phrase. Where does it come from, then? Is it pertinent in terms of biblical theology? In biblical use, *what* is "spread"?

If I am correct, the Luther-Bible, for example, uses the word only three times in the New Testament for actions of the disciples, and then in the sense of "spreading the word" or the message of Jesus (Mk. 7:36; Lk. 2:17; Acts 13:49). Nowhere is it said that the disciples spread the kingdom of God.

Now one might object that "spreading the kingdom of God" is only another formula for the Great Commission, which in Matthew

28 is contained in the words, "make disciples of all nations" (v. 19). But that is not true either. For Jesus' Great Commission proceeds from the presupposition, "all authority in heaven and on earth has been given to me," that is, under the presupposition of the factual worldwide existence of the kingdom of Christ. There is no need to spread the lordship of Christ; it already exists everywhere. "Make disciples" could only deal with the concrete *execution* of Jesus' worldwide lordship which has already been inaugurated. So if one wants to continue to use the idiom "spread the kingdom of God," for which there are perhaps good reasons, then one must remain constantly aware of the imprecision of this expression.

The text of the Lausanne Covenant, however, is talking here not just about a spread of the kingdom but of the "spread of the righteousness of the kingdom of Christ," that is, of a spread of the qualities or the *fruits* of the kingdom. According to all that has been said already, however, that is not directly possible. Rather one must conclude that whoever wants to spread the harvest of fruits must set out more new trees!

Through its context, moreover, the text of the article before us compels us to conclude just that. Shortly before, it says explicitly that it is by regeneration that one enters the kingdom of Christ and thus gains access to its righteousness. "Spread the righteousness of the kingdom of God" can, then, have only one meaning, namely, do not be content with your own realization of the righteousness of the kingdom of God, but help others to realize it also, that is, help them toward regeneration.

So beside the sanctification of one's own life this would be a matter of helping others to be born again with an ethical intent. That would be legitimate. But this would return us to the content of Article 4 which talks about evangelistic preaching for conversion. Perhaps the conclusion of Article 5 wants to say something else. But, then, it has not expressed it clearly.

The question still remains: of what does the righteousness of the kingdom of Christ consist? Certainly the answer must be: all the previously mentioned acts which comprise the Christian's social responsibility. It consists of reconciliation, liberation, respect for the dignity of man, service to people and the renunciation of opposite ways of behavior. This very thing must also be the content and goal of the Christian social and political activity which the middle sentence of Article 5 demands.

Beyond that we may think of Jesus' Sermon on the Mount, of the golden rule (Mt. 7:12), of the double commandment of loving God and neighbor (Mt. 22:37-40) and the exposition of the latter in Jesus' parable of the good Samaritan, as well as of the "fruit of the Spirit" of Galatians 5 and of the whole New Testament hortatory writings.

4

The Task
Ahead

First of all, it seems to me, we must keep in mind the biblical *corrections* which have been seen to be necessary in the phraseology of Article 5 of the Lausanne Covenant:[29]

1. There is a legitimate biblical meaning of "liberation," but it does not consist in the motto of Spartacus: self-help of the oppressed. The call for liberation, rather, is one part of the prophetic preaching for rulers to repent; specifically, it is a call to *emancipate* the oppressed.

2. There is, in fact, a "prophetic office of the church," which includes preaching repentance to society. But such a sermon, as we saw, does not take the approach of "denouncing evil" to others but the path of addressing the evildoers directly. The prophetic sermon is given to the rulers, not to the victims of the authorities. It seeks change within the rulers, not their liquidation. We saw that John the Baptist, for example, did not even question the usurped dominion of Herod but sought to bring him to God while in this position. He took the way of the prophet, not that of the zealot.

3. The righteousness of the kingdom of Christ cannot be "spread" in any other way than by a comprehensive "obstetrics"

for the regeneration of people. This certainly does not reject Christian cooperation in the structure by which creation is preserved. It occurs, however, on another level than that which the "righteousness of the kingdom of Christ" addresses.[30]

Beyond that, in my opinion, since Lausanne we need to address a series of tasks related to evangelical social ethics. Here are several fundamental ones:

1. With Padilla we must constantly stress that we have been commissioned with preaching a gospel—in evangelism and mission—which includes the call to a life of discipleship and following Jesus. Evangelism deals with repentance; and repentance, with ethics. The antithesis (even the subtle kind) between the doctrine of justification and ethics must be sent packing everywhere it is found.

The antithesis between eschatology and ethics, between hope and conduct, is just as unscriptural. When an evangelical missions conference (after Lausanne!) passionately prayed "Thy kingdom come" but not "Thy will be done on earth as it is in heaven," that was another characteristic abridgment of biblical teaching. Paul's desire to be with Christ by no means crippled his earthly activity; rather it spurred it on further (Phil. 1:21-26). The apostle did not just stand still in anticipation of joy, but compared his life with that of an Olympic competitor (1 Cor. 9:26-27). Neither justification nor hope motivates quietism in the New Testament; rather they motivate sanctification and diligent work in mission.

2. A further task in the direction of an evangelical social ethic is to balance evangelism as initial preaching of salvation with doctrinal, follow-up instruction. The evangelistic workers especially are obligated to see that those who become believers receive comprehensive Christian instruction. Otherwise, their own work itself is futile.

There is a great need here today. Look at the New Testament letters and what was expected of young Christians and young churches in doctrinal teaching and ethical instruction. Much would be better in modern Christianity if we would furnish the newly·won with such food in the future.

Doctrine is the duty of teachers, that is, the theologians. They, with others, have the vocation to be nourishers of the church (Mt. 24:45). The condition of theology today, however, by and large does not encourage the exercise of that task. Therefore, there must be a change of mind in theology so that it again serves the maintenance and development of the church. But where the teachers do not sufficiently fulfill their duty, the evangelists must jump in and take care of it.

3. The third task concerns social ethics itself. The quickly fleeting addresses of Lausanne and the stimulating, yet quite brief, Article 5 of the Lausanne Covenant before us do not yet make an evangelical social ethic. One must now be thought through and developed.

"Evangelical" can mean many things, as we well know, in the spectrum of denominations and tendencies. Bishop Lilje recently defined it this way: "The essential common mark [of the evangelical] is the determination to abide by the testimony of the biblical Christ."[31] If it be accepted that Christ stands in the center and Scripture is the authority, then we will have found a reliable platform.

But what is "social ethics"? Does Article 5 of the Lausanne Covenant actually deal with social ethics? Furthermore, is "social ethics" to be understood in such a way that what is social, the society, is the agent of conduct or rather that the society is the object of our own personal conduct? In ethics one must not only distinguish the principles and fields but also the agents of action. In social ethics are we thinking of instructions for society (for collective or communal agents of action, of laws and ordinances which they make), or of what the individual Christian or the Christian church does for society?

Article 5 obviously speaks in the second sense. This also seems to be indicated by the fact that, except for this article and a brief mention of "aid" (in Article 9 on the "Urgency of the Evangelistic Task"), nowhere else in the Lausanne Covenant is the duty of *diakonia* mentioned. It is *social diakonia* as an act of the Christian church that Article 5 actually talks about.

Therefore, in my opinion, what is to be said of social ethics in the first and second sense must be more carefully worked over.

Surely the Christian church will initially and primarily work in individual and social ministry (Jer. 29:7: "seek the welfare of the city ... "). But that does not exempt the church from the task of thinking through in advance on what grounds and in what way it legitimately can and should influence the conduct of society itself, say, in the formation of legal life. The abortion question is a relevant example for the urgency of this task.

4. In the framework of this social-ethical study the various models of Christian social service in the past and present should be collected for the mutual stimulation of Christians. No limits have ever been put on the imaginativeness of love. But we know too little of all that has already been accomplished under the leading of the Spirit. We must again make the church aware of the variety of models for Christian service, and we must make it aware of the task itself. We must—Escobar showed this at Lausanne—again pay attention to the neglected history of reforms, the existing great heritage of evangelical social work; we must study personalities, programs and results. I mention only Wesley, Wilberforce and Shaftesbury in whom modern social reforms recognizably developed out of revival.[32] I mention the Norwegian Hauge, and Wieselgren to whose Christian motivation the Swedish welfare state can be traced. I mention August Francke, the Alsatian Oberlin and Carl Mez of Baden—people about whom we today, unfortunately, get to read virtually nothing. In addition there is the whole history of Christian cooperatives which addressed the necessities of human life in regard to both production and consumption. Evangelicals have unjustly forgotten them.

So the fourth task consists in arousing awareness again of the church's task by collecting materials about these reformers and renewers of social life who were motivated by a biblical spirit. It will serve to stimulate the imagination regarding the manifold labors of maintaining life and all the many little, insignificant but concrete steps of vital aid which the great theoreticians of revolution always consider beneath their dignity but with which Christianity has shown itself to be the salt of the earth.

In this sense also the social-ethical article of the Lausanne Covenant could have been somewhat more concrete; it could have spoken of the tasks of protecting life, providing jobs, aiding refugees, granting freedom and social participation to the many foreign workers in the whole world.

In summary, the Lausanne Covenant, despite the aforementioned deficiencies, is a good stimulus to recover theoretically and practically what Christian social responsibility is and is not. It is good to hear once again biblically substantial arguments in this field instead of the prevalent secular ones. Article 5 of the Lausanne Covenant opens the way to a Christian ethic for the social realm which at the same time testifies to the authority of God's word. It points to a truly *theological* social ethic which the whole church needs today. "Theological existence today"[33]: this watchword also applies to the field of contemporary Christian social ethics.

Notes

[1]Emilio Castro, "Conversion and Social Transformation," *Christian Social Ethics in a Changing world*, ed., John C. Bennett, (New York and London: SCM, 1966), pp. 348-66. Compare my book, *Was heisst heute Mission? Entscheidungsfragen der neueren Missionstheologie* (Giessen and Basel: Brunnen, 1974), pp. 103ff.

[2]Compare Job 34:12: "and the Almighty will not pervert justice," as well as Jer. 9:24 and Ps. 99:4.

[3]Heb. 12:14, "strive for peace with all men," probably belongs here also.

[4]Compare Gal. 3:28; Col. 3:11; Eph. 6:8.

[5]On the following compare G. Fohrer, "*sozo and soteria* in the Old Testament," *Theological Dictionary of the New Testament*, ed. G. Friedrich, trans. and ed. G. W. Bromiley (Grand Rapids: Wm. B. Eerdmans, 1971), VII, 970-80, esp. 974f; and W. Foerster, "*sozo and soteria* in the New Testament," pp. 989-98. Foerster pointedly explains, "NT *soteria* does not refer to earthly relationships. Its content is not, as in the Greek understanding, well-being, health of body and soul. Nor is it the earthly liberation of the people of God from the heathen yoke, as in Judaism.... It has to do solely with man's relationship to God" (*Ibid.*, p. 1002).

[6]Compare Bockmuehl, pp. 17, 83.

[7]Karl Barth, *Church Dogmatics*, eds. G. W. Bromiley and T. F. Torrence, III, 4 (1951), trans. A. T. Mackay, T. H. L. Parker, H. Knight, H. A. Kennedy and J. Marks (Edinburgh: T. and T. Clark, 1961), p. 655.

[8]A. Schlatter, *Die Christliche Ethik*, 2nd ed., (Stuttgart: Calwer Verlag, 1929), pp. 162, 332.

[9]Barth, *Church Dogmatics*, II, 2 (1948), trans. H. Knight, G. W. Bromiley, T. K. S. Reid and R. H. Fuller (Edinburgh: T. and T. Clark, 1960), pp. 223f; and III, 4, pp. 653f.

[10]Also see Lev. 25:14. Greed wants to cheat.

[11]See 1 Cor. 5:10-11; 6:10; Eph. 4:19; 5:3, 5, etc., as well as Col. 3:5.

[12]See his significant paper "Der Dienst des Christen in der älteren Dogmatik" (1897), reprinted in A. Schlatter, *Zur Theologie des Neuen Testaments und zur Dogmatik*, ed. U. Luck *Theologische Bücherei*, (München: Chr. Kaiser, 1969), XLI, 31-105.

[13]See Gal. 6:10; 2 Thess. 2:13.

[14]See also Mt. 21:13; 23:37-39.

[15]Gerhard von Rad, *Theology of the Old Testament* (London: SCM Press), p. 36.

[16]*usus elenchthicus legis et evangelii*; the Latin phrase stands in the text of the original; the translation in the notes. Here they are reversed. (Tr.)

[17]A. Solzhenitzyn, "Open Letter to the Soviet Government," Spring, 1974, and most recently the manifesto of the Baptist preacher and professor Josef Ton in Rumania, "Die Stellung des Christen im Sozialismus," printed in the newsletter of the "Offensive junger Christen," Bensheim, No. 3-4 (1975), pp. 49-56, are among these famous exceptions.

[18]Billy Graham in his thoughtful opening address at Lausanne quoted the important missionary theologian Robert E. Speer. "We dare not confuse the *aim* of foreign missions with the *results* of foreign missions." By this he was thinking of social-ethical values. "It is a dangerous matter if we publicly before the whole world

set ourselves the task of reorganizing states and changing society," although that will be the effect of the new powers of the gospel. Graham and Speer relate this rejection of goal setting to social-ethical renewals. Do they perhaps also conceive of individual-ethical renewal only as an effect but not likewise an intention of preaching?

[19]This passage also has *hina* in the Greek.

[20]See especially the Heidelberg Catechism, Question 86; the Second Helvetic Confession, Chap. 16. The former is to be found in T. F. Torrance, ed., *The School of Faith* (New York: Harper & Brothers, 1959), pp. 86; the latter, in Philip Schaff, *Creeds of Christendom* (New York: Harper & Brothers, 1922), III, 864-68. In German see also "Apologie der Augsburgischen Konfession," *Bekenntnisschriften der evangelisch-lutherischen Kirche* (Göttingen; Vandenhoeck hg.v. Deutschen Evang. Kirchenausschuss, 1930), Chap. IV, pp. 197, 52.

[21]E. G. Selwyn, *The First Epistle of St. Peter* (New York: Macmillan, 1961), pp. 170, 373.

[22]A. Schlatter, *Der Evangelist Matthäus* (Stuttgart: Calwer Verlag, 1929), p. 150.

[23]Joachim Jeremias, *New Testament Theology*, tr. John Bowden (New York: Charles Scribner's Sons, 1971), p. 230.

[24]Theophil Spoerri, "Der Gemeindegedanke im ersten Petrusbrief," *Neutestamentliche Forschungen*, 2nd series, No. 2, ed., O. Schmitz, (Gütersloh: C. Bertelsmann, 1925), p. 65.

[25]A. Schlatter, *Petrus und Paulus nach dem ersten Petrusbrief* (Stuttgart: Calwer Verlag, 1937), p. 106.

[26]Karl Barth writes, "And if ever I come to fear lest mine is a case of self-hallucination, one glance at the secular events of those times, one glance at the widening circles of ripples in the pool of history, tells me of a certainty that a stone of unusual weight must have been dropped into deep water there somewhere." See "Biblical Questions, Insights, and Vistas" (1920) in *The Word of God and the Word of Man* (London: Hodder, 1928), p. 63.

[27]Schlatter, *Matthäus*, p. 255: "However, as the fruit grows from the branches and makes its inner and hidden life process visible, effects extend from the prophet which move others in their lives and these effects reveal the nature and origin of his word."

[28]Schlatter, *Die Christliche Ethik*, p. 44.

[29]It is noteworthy that all three critical concepts, the misconstruable concept "liberation" and the two useless concepts "denounce" and "spread" first got into the text of the Lausanne Covenant during the Congress.

[30]On this see my book *Conservation and Lifestyle*, tr. Bruce N. Kaye, Grove Booklets on Ethics, No. 20 (Bramcote: Grove Books, 1977), pp. 16f.

[31]Hans Lilje, *Memorabilia: Schwerpunkte eines Lebens* (Stein-Nürnberg: Laetare, 1973), p. 241.

[32]Richard Lovelace, *The Dynamics of Spiritual Life* (Downers Grove: InterVarsity Press, 1979).

[33]The title of a periodical series begun by Karl Barth and others to counter liberalism and the "German Christian" movement of the Nazi era. (Tr.)

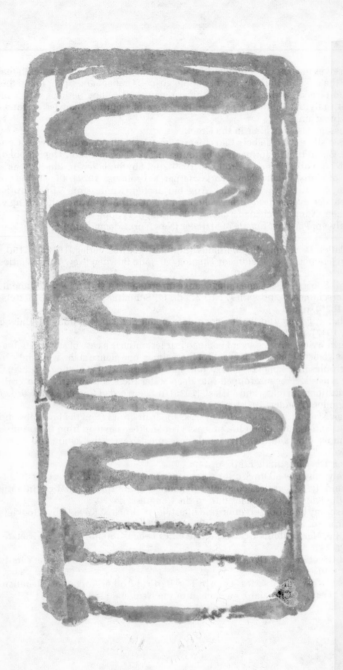